And What Would You Say If You Could?

THIRD MAN BOOKS

NASHVILLE, TENNESSEE

AND WHAT WOULD YOU SAY IF YOU COULD?

BY HAVILAND N.G. WHITING

For information:
Third Man Books, LLC, 623 7th Ave S, Nashville, Tennessee 37203.

A CIP record is on file with the Library of Congress

FIRST EDITION

Design and layout by Allison Poplett

Cover photo "Interior of Slave Cabin at Whitney Plantation, NOLA" by Haviland N.G. Whiting

ISBN: 978-1-7333501-0-5

To my parents: you have never stopped believing in me.

Table of Contents

Memory...1

The Forgetting...2

Migration..3

Sins of Our Fathers...4

Untitled I...5

The Storyteller...6

Katrina..7

Growing Pains...8

Foreword...9

Afterword...10

The Fire This Time...11

She Who Lit the Match in Mississippi.................................14

St. Louis Hotel...15

Bedtime Stories..16

Ave Maria...17

Interlude...18

A Re-imagination...19

Congo Square Where We Danced..20

Hunger...21

A Girl's First Love..22

Loss..23

At Least For Now...24

Lately...25

Consequence of Silence..26

Dear Stephanie..29

Bridge..31

Regret...32

Dear J.T...33

Untitled II...34

Cyntoia...37

On Immigration..38

Lessons...41

Preface

There is a polaroid film worn-away-at-the-edges kind of beauty about this nocturnal daydream. I see Venice at night, and Paris as sunlight comes in through the blinds. I smell twilight in Marrakech and taste the silence of New Delhi, and yet nothing compares to the roaring silence inside my own head. Where I write is noisy and incomprehensible. I think in music notes, and I let them flow out of me onto a cello fingerboard. I breathe in ballet and exhale a *pas de deux*. I write and I create to escape a world overrun with busy movement. I write to relax but I also write because I want to change the world. That comes later, though. I exist inside myself but also as a speck of light in the universe. I write because I know what it's like to change someone's day with a single word. Because I have had it happen to me, I believe in the power of the written word. That it is a cliché does not make it untrue. Touched by Sylvia Plath at the impressionable age of thirteen in a small college town at a summer camp in rural Massachusetts, I saw the world anew when in that same fall my mother gave me Warsan Shire's *Teaching My Mother to Give Birth* and M. NourbeSe Philip's *Zong!*. A family friend donated Claudia Rankine's *Citizen* and the little-known but extremely important 1981 anthology *Black Sister – Poetry by Black Women, 1746–1980*.

As my mentor, Thadious Davis, whose work is included in the aforementioned poetry collection, has written of Alice Walker's transition from poetry to fiction in her essay, "Poetry as a Preface to Fiction," fiction too has been a muse, a "preface" to my poetic imagination. The descriptions of the rituals of violence experienced by slave women as well as their resistance to dehumanization in Octavia Butler's *Kindred* and Marlon James's *Book of Night Women* revved my imagination. I love pretty, beautiful things. One day I would like to create beautiful things. The world and its past and present happenings are not always things of beauty. Racism. Sexism. Colorism. Slavery. Violence. Death. Yet, these often-unspeakable things are importantly spoken in the most beautiful but damning words.

Moonlight spreads over my cheek; I spread my notebook over the mahogany hotel desk where I composed this preface as a sort of introduction to me and what is to come in the following pages. Now I will return to the beginning; the genesis of my midnight escape.

Haviland Nona Gai Whiting
Rome, Italy,
June 22, 2019
2018 Nashville Youth Poet Laureate
2019 United States Youth Poet Laureate Ambassador

Memory

A girl slings her monogrammed backpack over her shoulder,
"I wish black people didn't have to make everything about race."
A pause,
"Yes," I reply,
"Me too."

The Forgetting

Black people bodies hidden away like America's younger cousin.
They sleep in the Mississippi and hide in the forest, in trees.
You hear trees whistlin' at night,
Ain't the crow or the lark.
It be the girls who can't sleep
For fear a white man use her bones as a necklace,
Her teeth like crowning jewels.

Migration

The water rusts the iron that breaks the backs
The blacks
The backs of barrels
Of rum and of guns
That kick and moan on the bow of the ship
Treading water
Swallowing water
Lungs, black backs and barrels
Black backs and scars that pass
Through family lines,
My blood line breathes water.
Swimming, is the body's way of expelling
And by that I mean a body
Remains untouched only when it is valuable.
In the market,
A girl my age is worth a hundred.
In another
She's worth 2.
Women learnt priding themselves
On how much money it takes
To spread their legs wide,
Same girl passed around
Till she forgets who owns the spaces
Grown men call "home,"
They
Go home to their wives
Covered in blood
Shame rocks his body at night
A witch, a black magic bitch
With candy between her thighs
The ship that never turns around
Like the sharks that devour,
Always swimming towards
A horizon that glimmers
Ready to swallow a body whole
As it sinks to the ocean
Floor.

Sins of Our Fathers

The prettiest girl on the market,
She, dark and strong
Skin glistening, ribs poking, mother drowning
In the sea.
The prettiest girl on the market,
Has hips too narrow for breeding,
But a body that's meant for sexing.
The other women look on,
In a grotesque admiration
Ain't nothin' special 'bout bein'
America's bitch.

Untitled I

Mama came back with 300 lashes
Clean across her back.
Her eyes rolled up,
So only a crescent moon could be seen
Blood ran down and up and sideways,
Three men and her hips
And rape was never a part of
A slave's vocabulary.
Mama was dying on the indigo field,
Freedom settled into her bones and she ran,
With Louisiana calling her back
Mama skin hang off her like a hand-me-down coat
I asked her,
Mama, what freedom taste like?
(I was but a girl, freedom but a fruit)

The Storyteller

Soft skin and dry paint
Coat the underside of his fingernails
Like grime in a high school bathroom,
Or a church.
How many women live
Under the claws of hungry wolves?

Katrina

Jazz music flutters up the balcony
As she takes a breath
Of the sweet scent of the city,
Rolling and writhing below.
A woman,
Begging for a dollar or two
Somethin' bout hard times
In Louisiana
We all just strugglin' to get by.
Looked up at the sky tonight,
Focused on a star and I asked it,
I said
(I says to it),
God, take all you want from me,
But please, let me keep my children.
So Katrina left
And took them, too.

Growing Pains

When I heard that a man drove his car around the campus,
Looking at little girls in their school skirts and Mary Janes
I asked Dad to take me to the range.

Girls, the muses of famous poets
We are honey, sweet tea, soft skin.
Girls are the moon.
The moon is only considered beautiful because she does not speak.

Girls, the only ones who can be locked behind a bookcase
Smothered in an attic,
Sent through the swamps of Louisiana
And still believe people are truly good at heart.

Girls who are taught to fawn over boys,
And we are just boy crazy, the way we drift
In pairs to the bathroom, or clutch keys in
Hand in empty movie theater garages.

I go to the shooting range with my father.
He teaches me how to hold a revolver, I tell him "I got this."
What I mean is
A teacher was fired for taking upskirt videos.
I aim.

Gunpowder smells like tampax and socks and blood and bile the
School locker room,
Locker room talk,
Nothing is ever mentioned
If it happens in a locked room.

My dad sees a paper target, I see a man entering into my room
His hand on my doorknob
Holding my windows shut.
I fire.

BLACK AND WHITE MISSISSIPPI
Photo: Haviland N. G. Whiting

Foreword

There is no reason why I can't stop writing about slavery, except for
the fact that I've realized scars are transmitted through families. No
black backs remain untouched. Maybe that is why.

Afterword

The mighty Mississippi rages like blood
Screaming and gushing
The slaves coagulated in the hold of the ship.
The slaves used to be people.
The Mississippi is where America forgets your name,
"The slaves"
And nothing before that.

The Fire This Time

"When the men come, set yourself on fire."–Warsan Shire

    1. On the first day of war or maybe it was religion, god
said to carry bullets under our tongues. He said, these men
will try to swallow your holy. He said, I'll protect you, and
shrouded us in cloaks called skin. Eve said, how beautiful it
is to be wearing the night.

    2. On the second day of beauty, Eve plucked an apple from
the tree lifted it to her lips; god said, stop, that's strange
fruit. Eve folded up her ammunition tongue and forgot what
it meant to be holy.

    3. On the last day of love or maybe it was regret, Eve allowed
Adam to mispronounce "woman." He looked at her, fruit juice
running down his chin; said, I've never been with a black wom-
an before. Strange fruit. Forbidden fruit. Eve said, my body has
been divided into cities. My lungs are refugee camps. My thighs
are borders. But oh god, don't I wear the World well?

These cloaks wear our mother's curse
Slipping into this skin dress
With shackles like special occasion pearls.
Girlhood is the forbidden fruit,
Biting into beauty like barbed wire.
Spilling sorry like an accident,
Like a cut tongue.
Constantly forced to apologize for femininity.

For too long, Black women have been
Hiding our ammunition tongues.
Boxing up our bodies like cargo
But what I am saying is we are cargo
By now, we're expected to know that, though.

Bodies float, bodies hang, bodies
Shipped from continent to continent,
26 girls who were
Always more angel than human.
Always more Delilah than Mary
Samson mistaking her shrinking for permission,

There is no one to give
Skin a burial at sea.
The loneliest cemetery is the pause
After the kickback.
Semi automatically assuming
Slavery ended when the last fruit was eaten.

Kill the mind, feed the body,
Youth is a concept
Most black girls know like water
Which is to say we all need it
Drinking even as we're drowning.
Even as we're screaming
Even as we're Cyntoia Brown-ing
Even after we've trained our tongues to say
Home is the skin at the back of our closets.
Wearing black girlhood as a noose

Black women are often victims of sexual abuse
The silence kills more of us daily
And the blood is often just used as war paint.
The female body is
A loaded gun,
Maybe that's why
We're debating gun control

To be woman and to be black
Is to know that your beauty does not belong to you,
Is to be the first and last person to love yourself.
You grow up learning to protect the men who hate you.
To know that silence is
Your most viable weapon.

Somewhere, Moses is parting a girl's legs
Like the seas we see as grave sites.
Gun control,

Is leaving the safety on
If it means he can't get in.

She Who Lit the Match in Mississippi

The lone abortion clinic in Mississippi stands like a Pepto-Bismol
dismal reminder of the girls who fight to call their bodies their own.
Outside the streets are littered with spray paint cans, tobacco, and
broken glass. The protestors hold up images of mangled fetuses as
if the fifteen-year-old girl did not cry herself clean in the shower.
Nothing you will show me, her shaking shoulders seem to scream,
will baptize me as well as my own blood already has.

St. Louis Hotel

"White people walk around like they shit don't stink"
Like they ain't got skin under they nails,
Fingernails in they teeth.
They got body parts
(All mixed up)
Cotton stained with blood looks like ink,
Black people blood look like the ink
They never learned to write with
(They always did, the books were burned)
They got sleep,
In hotels marked by slave-sin
Paint and bleach and bones,
(Will never CHANGE what you did)

Bedtime Stories

Have you forgotten
Who gave you your thumbs and lungs and statues?
Have you forgotten
Who built your church and mausoleum and morgue?
Did you forget
Whose hips you exited,
Screaming like a newborn, all in red?
Did you forget whose bed you rocked,
When your wife's grew too cold for the rum on your bones?
Did you forget whose hair you pulled,
Till you made a bracelet of "girl,"
Have you forgotten
Whose bodies you visit at night,
Whose scent you crave?
Who you forced to be "erotic"
Before she entered puberty?

Ave Maria

My mother taught me to cook,
That was her mistake.
Los frijoles, los negros, la plancha
The power has been out for weeks
The freezing, la caldera, the heating
Glass enters skin like sweat forms on upper lips under wide brim hats.
The windows are busted in, that's why there's glass
It is easier to pretend glass
Is the only thing white people left behind,
"Los americanos come to build a hotel here."
Wind passes through the house
In January,
Here, it is easier to pretend the stars will bring humanity back,
And Maria is still a virgin.
The water poured in through the windows,
And the front door.
It stained the carpet,
And molded the ceilings.
It shattered my abuelita's ribs,
And left us all parched.
I dream of the thing that took my family.

Interlude

We are only a moment.
At midnight, a bottle of purple hair dye
The highway reflected off your fingernails.
You watch the cars flying by too closely.
I cling to you,
You grab the overpass.
"Come on. Don't you want to know what it feels like to be great?"

A Re-imagination

My great aunt holds a porcelain unicorn figurine in her left hand,
She stirs the soup on the stove
With the other.
She asks me,
"Child, what are you just sittin' there fo'?"
The room smells like chicken broth.
Below the house
There are boxes and bins
Of memories.
A rabbit in a green dress.
A bundle of piano keys.
I sit and try to hear the music.
After returning to the house wearing different shoes and a different height,
The kitchen smelled like empty air.
The footsteps were still.
"She's dying," Momma said,
"Go say goodbye."
A rose,
Given to me by an old man
On the street corner
Found its way to her breast.
Her hands were mottled then
Like the skin of the chickens
She used to cook.
Her hair was thinner then,
Like my legs at the time.
She didn't speak or make any noise,
Like the piano keys in the basement.
That rose slowed her heartbeat.
I took the rabbit in the green dress,
But let the other memories sleep.

CONGO SQUARE, NEW ORLEANS, LOUISIANA
Photo: Haviland N. G. Whiting

Congo Square Where We Danced

In Congo Square at night, you can still see them dancing. The *pat
pat* or the *moribayassa* or the *sway* and *sing and glide*. Hands up (to
god) and a dance all together. The rhythm sails through the trees
like a lark, and they still dancing. If you hold your breath, you can
smell the sweat. This sweat thick with love and human touch. Blood
dries in the square. Murdered babies come alive in the square.
Husbands and wives make love in the square. Hold your breath till
you pass out in the square. Ain't none of it real but the trees.

Hunger

In Jamaica, the trees can talk.
They sing a song for the mouths that hang,
Open in a silent scream or a silenced scream,
The trees don't know, they only sing.
The old sugar mill falling apart,
The ghosts that live in the rafters look out over the Atlantic,
They pour sugar into the waves,
Into their palms,
They never eat the sugar.
Black people never allowed the sweetness.

A Girl's First Love

When a woman loves herself,
She reorganizes the way the world works.
When she takes off her clothes
Before a shower and
Admires her thighs,
The way her skin glows,
All of her body hair.
When she runs a finger over her lips,
A hand over her hips,
When she paints her stretch marks on
Like fissures in a grand mountain.
When she carves out her glass ribcage
And shatters it like expensive crystal
When she runs a hand through her hair
Or over her scalp,
When she feels the strength in her teeth
And her eyelashes capable
Of catching tears,
And when she loves herself
So completely
And so wholly,
A woman can redesign the solar system,
And call herself a star.

Loss

And then I say, "What if he leaves as soon as you have given him everything? If you give him your body he takes your mind, too you know? What if he leaves?"

She stares at the ceiling, which is yellow in some places. "Yes, but what if he doesn't?"

At Least For Now

He is mentioned not by his name or the sound of his voice
But by the graciousness of his smile,
The rainforests swimming behind watery eyes,
By the way we laugh
And all of the strange places we find ourselves.
I do not love him because it is easy
But like sunlight over swimming pools,
Or leaking through the leaves
Because this life would have it
No other way.

Lately

Lately I've been having trouble differentiating between being
Whole and being happy.
It's like constantly apologizing
To god because your prayers
Went unanswered,
Or your shoes went untied
And you tripped.
Even though he told you
To tie your shoes,
First.
And so lately I've been wondering
If I can be happy
Even if I keep tripping over my own laces.
Even if I'm the one
Hindering my own happy,
Swallowing my own sunshine
Or handing it to someone else.
Being a whole person means
You never lost the sad parts,
The hard parts,
The driving in your car off the road
Into a tree parts.
The steering wheel feels like a trigger parts.
The forgetting the part.
I don't want to be whole all of the time.
A half person is answered
By god on the first ring,
I'm always being sent to voicemail.

So I decide maybe to walk without shoes.
To drive with no steering wheel,
To remove anything that could hurt me except I'm always still here.
I'm always still here
And I never learned how to tie my own shoes or how not to fire a gun at myself—
Defense tactic is protecting myself
From myself.

Consequence of Silence

It's 1.
I'm checking the lock on the door,
She's running water in the sink.
The sky is rosy with summer glow.
We laugh,
Allow August to thaw her heart-
Break is a funny thing
A reminder that people are here forever
Until they're not
Until, Autumn arrives.
With every snapping branch, I feel
Her hands grow colder
Until one day I reach for them and there's just
Ice makes the ground slick
While I call the helpline.
The woman who answers has a voice
Like melted honey.
Her voice is like summer while
I'm trapped in
Winter
Comes too quickly.
She hasn't eaten in days,
Nothing but tea
Which she brews with the bags under her
Eyes.
My winter girl.
Fine porcelain and teacups,
White paper and black pen.
The letter that you will write me
Will be born in the winter.
I take your hand again, tell you
That everything will be

Okay is a myth.
I've learned through seeing

My best friend eat herself alive
That living
Is the suicide of the mind.
I know if she records a tape,
My name will be first.
I stand, waiting with my hands outstretched.
I wait for her to come to bed.
My winter girl is walking down the hall,
I ask if she's locked the door.
She runs bath water
I wait for summer to come.

When spring arrives,
She's wearing a new shade of skin.
Having swallowed her old one, she is
Sleeping soundly on her side.
April is visiting quietly, the curtains
Are swaying in the breeze.
I take note of every laceration on her wrist,
I take note of her thinning waist and her
Thinning hair.
I say nothing.
I know my name will be the first on the tape.
I want to bring her soup and water as if
This is a common cold,
As if winter doesn't stick to the roof of my mouth
Like blood.
But this is a flu. She starves.

It's summer again.
The sky is orange at 2 am.
The world ended mid-July.
I'm writing this letter two years too late.
Two voicemails too late
You never left a tape or a note,
But I know my name was first.
My winter girl,
Like an unfamiliar relative

These words took years to arrive,
My porcelain and paper girl

I'm writing you into memorial
Before you're even gone,
Trying to fit my pain into computer code
Enter: me
Output: you
Command:
Hurting, hurting, hurting
Public static and avoid

Output:

Did you check the lock on the
Door?

Dear Stephanie

According to WebMD
There are five stages of grief.
Denial, anger, bargaining, depression, acceptance.

Today, I went to lay flowers
Where your footprints used to invite the springtime.
The sun has finally come out,
And the wind carries the scent.
Any second now,
I expect you to emerge from your office
Hair coiffed
Smile tailor made just for me.
I expect you to walk through those doors
And I expect you to be in the audience
When I recite a poem
About how much I miss you since you
Since you
And still, I'm staring
Grief in the face like the last candle
To burn out.
Sickness is a quiet killer.
I will plant you a garden of roses
And hydrangeas and poppies
I'm angry
I never got to ask what your favorite flower is.
I wish I could write a better poem.
I wish I could write a better poem with stanzas strong enough to build you a palace.
At least I asked God
To make you a star
So that we may wish on
You when the night is too dark
Dear Stephanie,
You used to fold up our doubts and fears and fly them away like paper planes.
You used to have hands large enough to support this whole school.
You used to walk into rooms and paint the walls Happy.

People like you don't just Die.
Energy can never be destroyed,
Only created in different forms
You pass on.
Death is not the absence of life
In a body
But that a body can no longer contain
That much love.

Bridge

"If you could talk to dead people," she hesitates, then "what would you tell them?"
"What?"
"Like, what would you say if you could?"
There's a pause, and soon,
The question is forgotten.

Regret

Once he has tasted honey,
He will never go back to kissing bees;
Knowing that the sweetest substance
Is in the rose he left behind.

Dear J.T.

Your father was the kind of a man
Who wrapped money up in baby blankets
Swaddled secrets in bodies
Bottled broken hearts in empty cans of corona.
Your father was flicker spit,
Doused in water,
He burned himself down.
Your father was the absence felt at
Every baseball game or basketball tryout.
He was the loudest silence between
Applause that never came from him,
Your father was the kind of man whose absence was his presence.
Always more ghost than skin and bone.
He was a baker, an entrepreneur,
Always on business trips
That's why he was never around.
Your father was an engineer,
Creating the newest gadgets that sold like silver.
When he died,
They told you your father was a drug addict
Your father drank like Dionysus,
Stretched himself like Elijah,
Until he was powder
Inhaled then exhaled.

But you will remember
Elijah stretched himself to resurrect his son,
Dionysus poured wine over the body of his baby.
Your father and his absence were present
At every baseball game, every basketball tryout.
You will remember slipping into his chalk outline like a winter coat.

They will tell you that a drop of water
Extinguished the ghost of your father.
But to you, he will always be
A forest fire.

Untitled II

A boy walks home alone at night.
The city sprawls in all directions,
The pavement blacker than the night sky.
He walks
And he is walking.
And he calls his mother
To tell her he's on his way home.
And he is walking.

His pace quickens as lights illuminate
The pavement creating red shadows
On his blue-black skin,
He thinks of everything
He's ever done wrong:
Well he skipped school two days ago,
He snuck out to see his friends,
He took a candy bar from a gas station.
He runs.
And he is running.

And now the car has stopped
But its headlights still swallow the stars.
The boy calls his mom
To let her know he's on his way home
Except he isn't and he doesn't,
He fiddles with the iPhone.
He places an emergency call
And here's where he remembers
911 is not here to protect him anymore.

Don't shoot.
He is standing now.
In the middle of the street.
There is only silence
And he is standing.

His face is illuminated
Like the American flag
As if this moment
Is the most patriotic he has ever been,
Hands are sliding into waistbands now.
He is laying on the ground now.
There is still no one around,
He yells to his mother that he is just
On his way home.

A boy dies before arriving home that night.
A system of injustice
His back, the target practice.
The people of the city
Do not allow his blood to be cleaned away.

They do not allow
The very same water hoses
That haunted their children in 1963
To erase his memory.
His mother guards their home at night.
She is saintly now,
With caverns under her eyes.
His father cries on live television.
A full grown man sobbing
Brings the crowd to their feet.

Somewhere,
The two officers who followed him home
That night turn off the news
And whisper self defense.
Self defense as if murder wears a disguise
When pronounced by white lips.

We miss the people we lose at night.
Brutality is a symptom of
An excess of power.
We have allowed it to swallow

Our children whole.
We try to forget the choices
We make at night.

Cyntoia

She woke up gasping,
Remembering how you stole her breath,
And force-fed it back to her.
Before she was ready to breathe
Again.

On Immigration

When the body of a little boy
Washed up on the beach,
I was sure the city was burning.
A refugee boat capsized in the Mediterranean
Killing all of the travelers.

These cities are burning,
The picture of his body tattooed
Itself to my eyelids
I see the world on fire, now
The word "refugee"
Sounds like the roaring sea now.

Watch, how we see now
That the only time brown bodies
Are on the news are when their breath has been
Stolen by the sea, now.

Here, cities do not burn.
They have been on fire for years
And the people are
Bruised, starved, shot
But they are still standing
A city can only be burning if it is disappearing
And in Aleppo,
The church is an empty coffin now
It holds no bodies now.

God is calling for his children now
Black Jesus is digging through the wreckage for hope now,
One day if the water washes through
And turns the city white,
One day if every-body that used to tuck its dreams into bed
Are washed out now
Then maybe we will help him
Look for them.

Here, brown bodies are a flare gun
On the stillest night.
A flare gun is supposed to signify
A person in distress
But how can you look at a gun and not panic.
How can you look at a black body
And not start searching for the Bible in your coat
Or a taser or a paper bag, now.

These cities will not burn
Notice how wherever you go,
Skin has become a warning sign,
A price tag
A brown girl may use the rock of the bow of a ship as a lullaby,
May familiarize herself with the men who took her mother.
War torn nations is what we call these places.

These places where a body is a broken thing and the religion has no
place in the alphabet.
But the other day in New York I swear
I heard a group of Latina girls
Were found dead
Isn't it funny
How these things only happen in war torn nations, now.
How gunfire can replace drums, now.
We are building walls now,
So we can't see suffocation on the other side.
There are broken families on the other side.
We are so scared of the other side,
We will bomb the other side.
Leave the city burning
To escape the broken English
On the other side.

Isn't it funny
How a tongue not used to speaking
A language is more dangerous than a body laying still on the beach?

The girl in my first period English class says "immigrant" like a dirty word.

I want to tell her that immigration is the way the world breathes.
Whether you speak to a brown person
With a mouth full of guns or a mouth full of fences,
Remember a city may burn itself to the ground,
The hospital may stink of forgetting,
The sky, a fireworks show for corpses.

But people are the mortar in the foundation,
Long after the bombings the bricks will still stand.
Puerto Rico, Aleppo, New York City,
Burning.

What do you remember about the earth,
When there is only water?
Forgetting is so easy
When home is a dangling appendage.
Where did you come from?
Will you go back?
I want to begin –
What is it like to begin?

Lessons

Look at the sun,
How she dresses herself in gold every morning.
She does not care if the moon sees her.
She is lovely for herself,
Only.

Acknowledgements

I'd like to thank Benjamin Smith and Southern Word for nurturing my writing and giving me the confidence to share it. Chet Weise and the team at Third Man Books, thank you for believing in my work. My mentor, Thadious Davis, has a special place in my heart and in the creation of this poetry collection. The faculty and administration at Harpeth Hall school also deserve special mention for allowing me the creative space during Winterim 2019 to develop some of the poetry published in this collection. To my dear friends, thank you for supporting me and encouraging me to write. Thank you for always serving as my muses, and having the integrity and vulnerability that inspires me to write. To my parents, I love you. You are the reason I did not give up on writing. To the art of poetry: thank you for the escape and the haven you have provided me. I promise not to waste it. And thank you to the readers and the listeners, who believe in the power of words.

HAVILAND N. G. WHITING, VENICE, ITALY 2019
Photo: Gilman W. Whiting

Born in New York and raised in Nashville, Haviland Nona Gai Whiting is
a 2019 United States Youth Poet Laureate Ambassador, the 2019 Southeast
Region Youth Poet Laureate, a 2019 Semi-Finalist for The National Student
Poets Program—a collaboration of the Institute of Museum and Library
Services and the Alliance for Young Artists & Writers, the 2018 Nashville
Youth Poet Laureate, and a 2018-2019 recipient of the Dr. Martin D. Jenkins
Scholar Award for Highly Talented and Gifted Black Children from the
National Association of Gifted Children. She sits on the Nashville Mayor's
Youth Council, in addition to participating in the Global Scholars Program at
the Harpeth Hall School for girls and young women where she is in her senior
year. In 2019, Haviland won the Scholastic Art & Writing Award Silver Medal
for Poetry as well as an Honorable Mention for Fiction, and a 2018 Gold
Medal. She was awarded the Concours National de Français Silver Medal by
the American Association of Teachers of French. Her work appears in *Nashville
Arts Magazine* and in *At Least I Know My Neighbor's Name: 2019 National
Youth Poet Laureate Anthology* published by Penmanship Books. An honor roll
student, Haviland is the First Chair Cello in Harpeth Hall's Upper School
Orchestra, serves as a school student ambassador, a staff writer for LOGOS,
the Harpeth Hall School student newspaper, and contributes literary works
to *Hallmarks: Art & Literature from the Upper School*. In her spare time, she
pursues photography, ballet, and is represented by AMAX Models.

The Nashville Youth Poet Laureate is a joint program of the Office of the Mayor, Metro Arts: Nashville Office of Arts + Culture, Nashville Public Library, Nashville Public Library Foundation, Urban Word, and Southern Word. The Nashville Youth Poet Laureate program aims to identify young writers and leaders who are committed to civic and community engagement, diversity and tolerance, and youth voice across Nashville.

CPSIA information can be obtained
at www.ICGtesting.com
Printed in the USA
LVHW082306061219
639668LV00007B/11/P